MY FIRST ACTIVITY BOOK

DRAW + LEARN
ANIMALS

by Harriet Ziefert   BLUE APPLE   Art by Tanya Roitman

Published in the United States 2011 by
Blue Apple Books, 515 Valley Street, Maplewood, NJ 07040
www.blueapplebooks.com
04/12   Printed in Shenzhen, China
ISBN: 978-1-60905-094-8

2 4 6 8 10 9 7 5 3

Draw your face.

Draw a circle.

 **Draw** a circle to make a face.

A face has eyes.

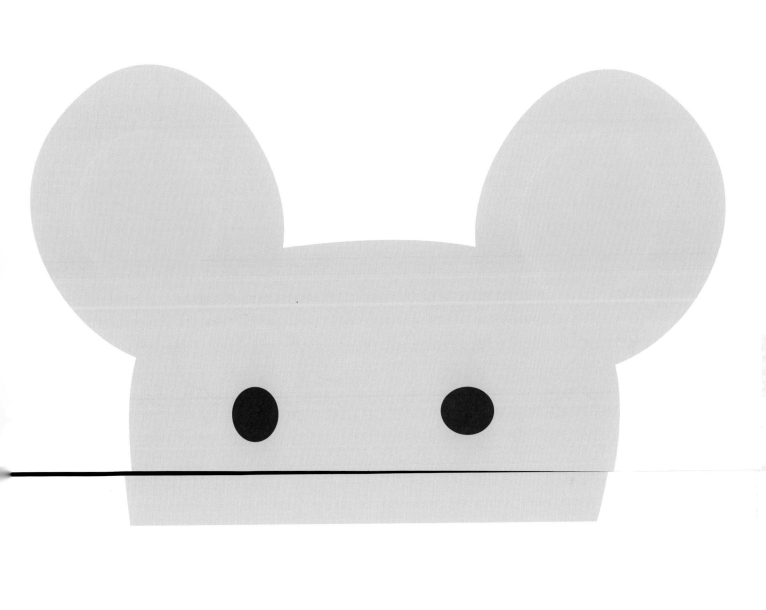

Eyes have eyelashes.

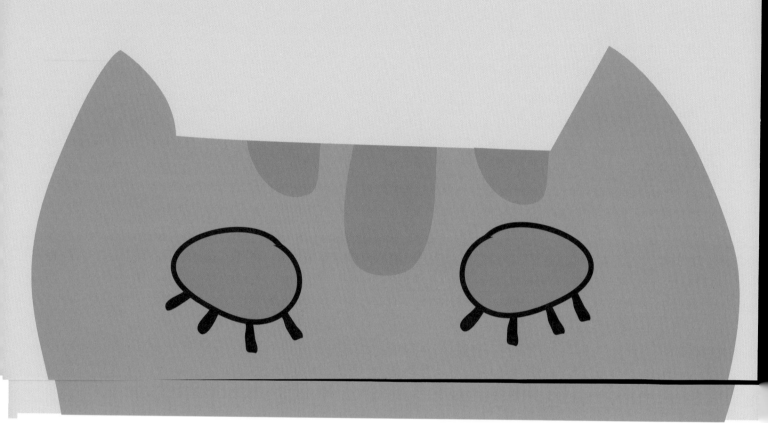

Draw the eyes.

A face has a mouth.

Bugs have faces.

 **Draw** the ladybug's face.

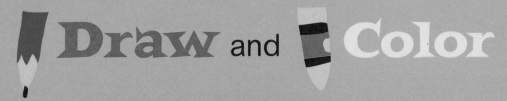

Make both halves the same.

Color the ladybugs.

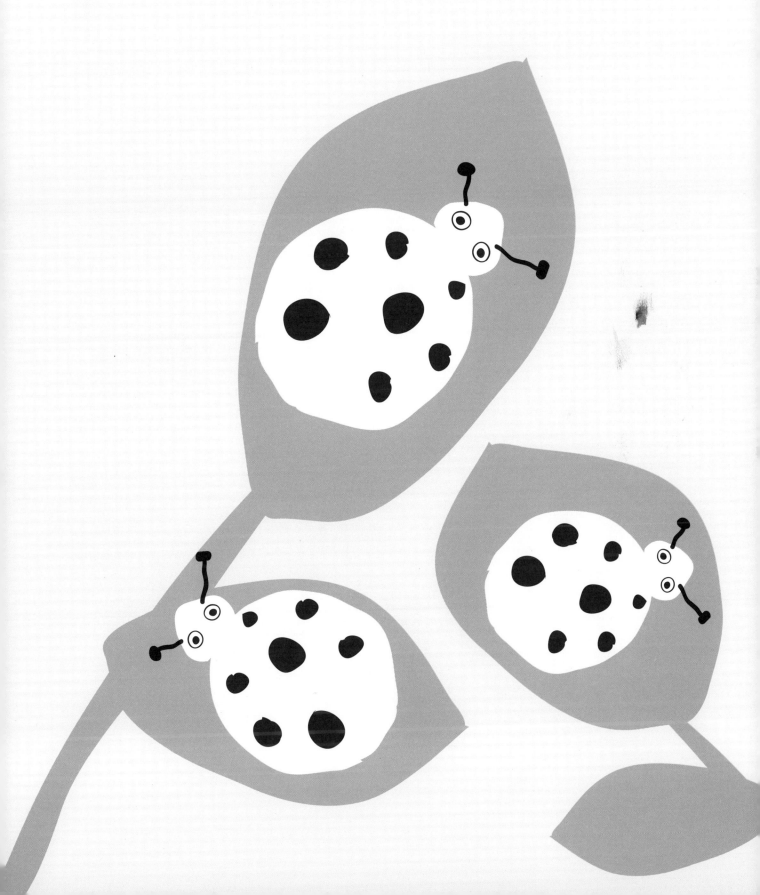

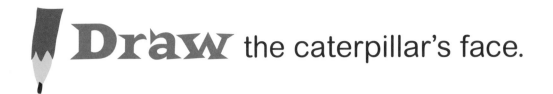 **Draw** the caterpillar's face.

 Color

 **Draw** eyes and a mouth.

 **Color** the ants.

 **Draw** eyes.

 Color

 **Draw** eyes.

 **Color** the cat.

Draw eyes.

 Color

 **Color** the chicks.

 **Draw** eyes.

Color the birds.

 **Draw** eyes.

 **Color** the birds.

 **Draw** eyes.

 Color

 Color

Dogs have eyes, a nose, and a mouth.

Draw what's missing.

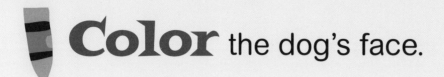 **Color** the dog's face.

 **Draw** a dog's face.

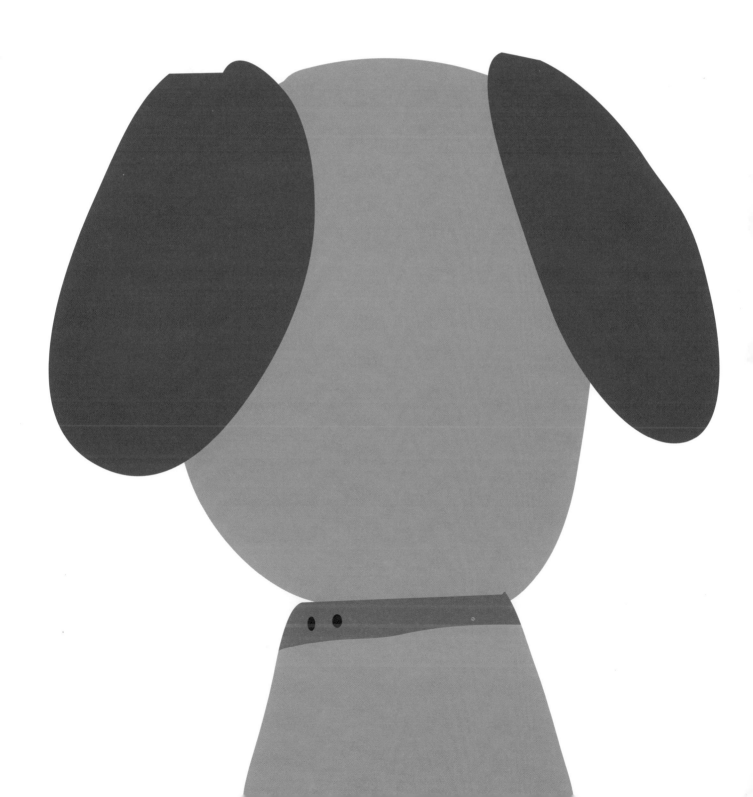

 **Draw** what's missing.

 # Color

Draw faces.

 Color

Color the big fish.

 **Draw** faces.

Color

Draw faces.

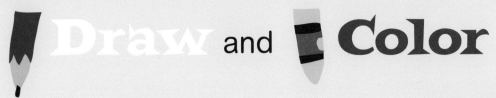 **Draw** and **Color**

Make both halves the same.

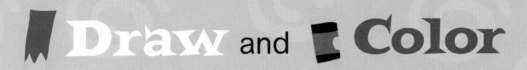

Make both halves the same.

Draw what's missing.

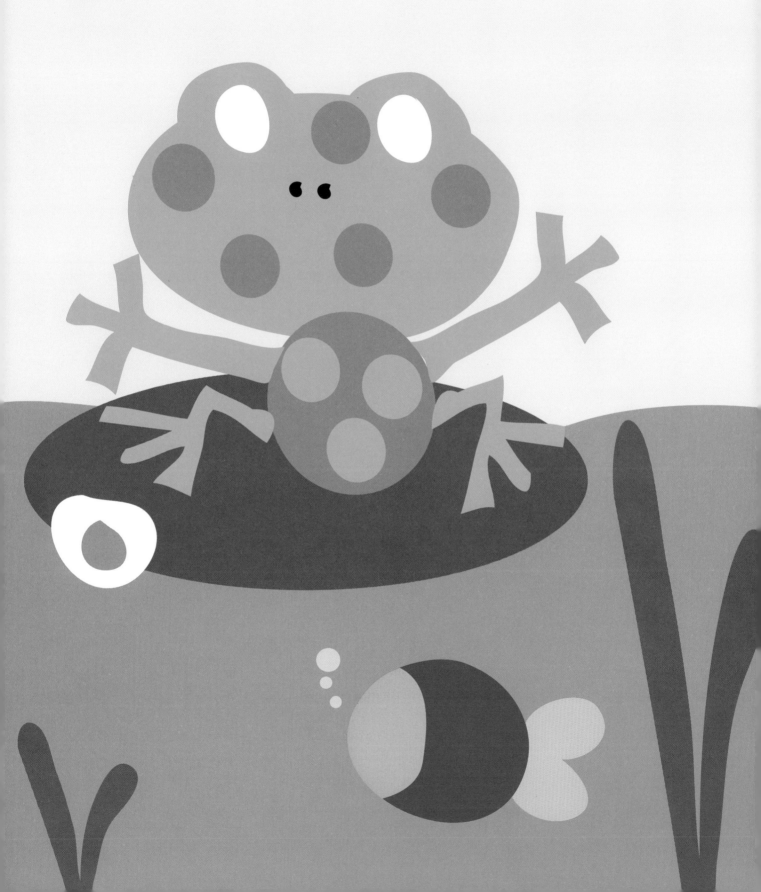

 Color

Draw and Color

Make both halves the same.

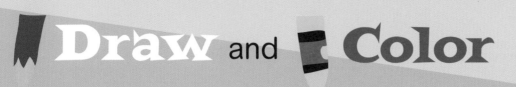 # Draw and Color

Make both halves the same.

Draw and **Color**

Make both halves the same.

Draw what's missing.

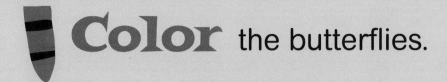 **Color** the butterflies.

 Color

Draw what's missing.

Draw what's missing.

 **Draw** what's missing.

Draw what's missing.

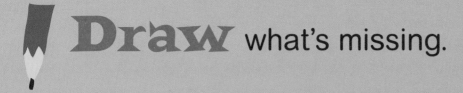 **Draw** what's missing.

Draw what's missing.

Draw what's missing.

 **Draw** what's missing.

Color the balls of yarn.

Color

 # Color

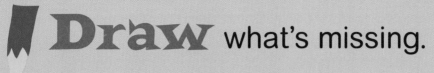

Draw what's missing.

Color the bear's body.

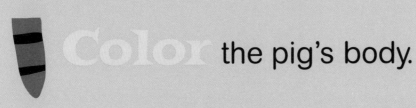 **Color** the pig's body.

Draw what's missing.

Color

 **Draw** a cat's face.

 **Draw** what's missing.

 **Draw** what's missing.

Draw what's missing.

Color

Animals have mouths.

 **Draw** what's missing.

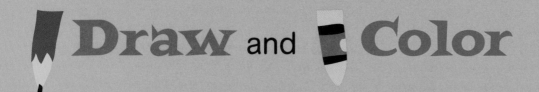

Draw and Color

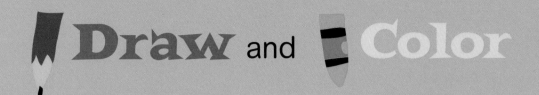

Draw and **Color**

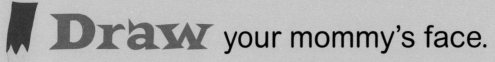 **Draw** your mommy's face.

Draw your daddy's face.

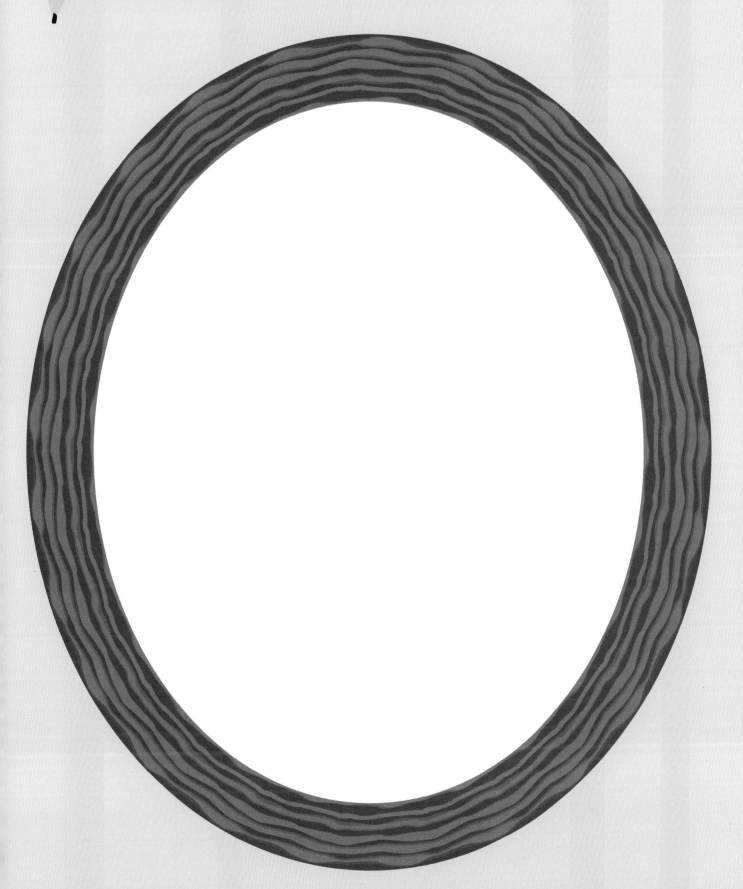

 **Draw** your face.